Big Data
Analyst

Other titles in the *Cutting Edge Careers* series include:

Biomedical Engineer

Cybersecurity Analyst

Robotics Engineer

Software Engineer

Video Game Designer

Virtual Reality Developer

Big Data Analyst

Bradley Steffens

San Diego, CA

© 2018 ReferencePoint Press, Inc.
Printed in the United States

For more information, contact:
ReferencePoint Press, Inc.
PO Box 27779
San Diego, CA 92198
www.ReferencePointPress.com

LIBRARY OF CONGRESS CATALOGING-IN-PUBLICATION DATA

Name: Steffens, Bradley, 1955– author.
Title: Big Data Analyst/by Bradley Steffens.
Description: San Diego, CA: ReferencePoint Press, [2017] | Series: Cutting Edge Careers series | Audience: Grade 9 to 12. | Includes bibliographical references and index.
Identifiers: LCCN 2017001817 (print) | LCCN 2017006547 (ebook) | ISBN 9781682821763 (hardback) | ISBN 9781682821770 (eBook)
Subjects: LCSH: Mathematics—Vocational guidance—Juvenile literature. | Mathematicians—Juvenile literature. | Big data—Juvenile literature.
Classification: LCC QA10.5 .S74 2017 (print) | LCC QA10.5 (ebook) | DDC 519.5/35023--dc23
LC record available at https://lccn.loc.gov/2017001817

CONTENTS

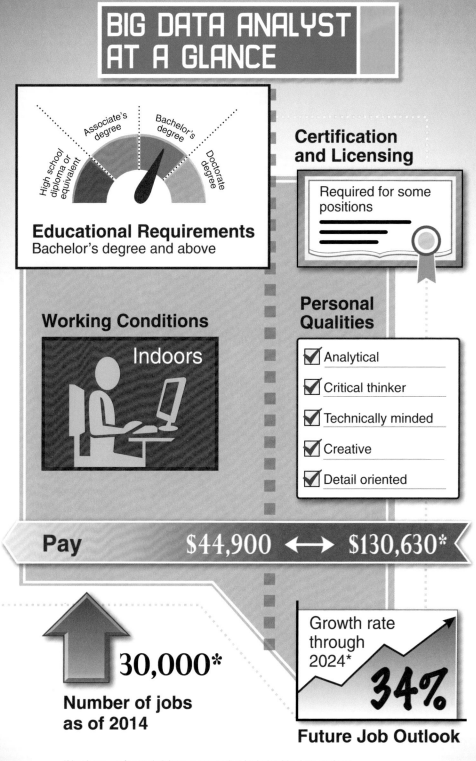

BIG DATA ANALYST AT A GLANCE

Educational Requirements
Bachelor's degree and above

High school diploma or equivalent · Associate's degree · Bachelor's degree · Doctorate degree

Certification and Licensing
Required for some positions

Working Conditions
Indoors

Personal Qualities
☑ Analytical
☑ Critical thinker
☑ Technically minded
☑ Creative
☑ Detail oriented

Pay $44,900 ⟷ $130,630*

30,000*
Number of jobs as of 2014

Growth rate through 2024*
34%
Future Job Outlook

*Numbers are for statisticians, a group that includes big data analysts.

Source: Bureau of Labor Statistics, *Occupational Outlook Handbook*, 2015. www.bls.gov.

Discovering Meaning in Digital Data

Digital devices generate vast quantities of data every day. IBM, the multinational technology company headquartered in Armonk, New York, estimates that 90 percent of all the data that exists in the world today was created in the last two years alone. This data comes from a variety of sources. Some of it is produced by machines, such as hospital equipment used to monitor patients, surveillance cameras that keep watch over buildings, and sensors used to gather information about pipelines or the electric grid. Some data comes from outer space, including weather satellites that track storms, spy satellites that eavesdrop on terrorists, and space probes that observe distant worlds. For example, during its twelve-year mission to the comet 67P/Churyumov-Gerasimenko, the *Rosetta* spacecraft sent thousands of digital images and millions of instrument readings back to Earth. "Rosetta has returned reams of data we are only beginning to analyze,"[1] said Mark McCaughrean, a senior science adviser at the European Space Administration.

However, the majority of digital data comes from human beings right here on Earth and is created when they e-mail, text, and post content to social media. For example, consider that each day Twitter users post 500 million tweets, Instagram users post 42 million photos, YouTube users upload 432,000 hours of video, and Facebook users share 4.75 billion pieces of content. This enormous quantity of information is known as big data.

Much of the data generated by both machines and humans would seem to have limited value. For example, a reading taken by a pipeline sensor one minute will be replaced by a newer, more relevant reading taken a minute later. Similarly, a Facebook "like" or comment might be seen by a few hundred people and then forgotten shortly thereafter. However, some computer experts, known as big data analysts, look at such information differently. A comment or like by one Facebook user might not be important, but put together, the reactions and opinions of Facebook's 1.79 billion active monthly users can yield meaningful information, revealing patterns of interests in people, products, and social movements. "The digital universe astronauts among us—the CIOs [chief information officers], data scientists, digital entrepreneurs—already know the value that can be found in this ever-expanding collection of digital bits," write John Gantz and David Reinsel, authors of the annual Digital Universe study published by International Data Corporation (IDC), a provider of market intelligence. "Hence, there is excitement about Big Data technologies."[2]

A Big Data Trick Provides a Halloween Treat

Since good information can lead to better sales and more efficient operations, large businesses have been among the first to analyze big data. One of the first to do so was Walmart. With more than $470 billion in annual revenue, Walmart is the world's largest retailer. The company's eleven thousand stores generate an astounding 1 million customer transactions every hour, all of which are tracked by big data analysts using specially designed computer software.

To understand what big data analysis offers companies like Walmart, consider the following story. In the days leading up to Halloween in 2015, Walmart's big data team noticed that cookies decorated with jack-o-lanterns, ghosts, and witches were selling well in most stores but not in others. The analysts contacted the stores where the Halloween cookies were not selling. The local merchandising teams discovered that the novelty cookies were actually still in the warehouses, not out on the shelves. Once store employees put the cookies on display, they sold out. The situation was easily resolved, but only because the big data analysts identified the problem quickly. "If you can't get insights until you've analyzed your sales for a week or a month, then you've lost sales within that time," says Walmart senior statistical analyst Naveen Peddamail. "Our goal is always to get information to our business partners as fast as we can, so they can take action and cut down the turnaround time."[3]

A Career with a Big Future

Because of big data's ability to help companies increase their sales and lower their costs, thousands of companies are launching big data operations. According to a 2015 survey conducted by the market research firm Gartner, more than 75 percent of private companies were investing or planning to invest in big data analysis in the next two years. Government offices, nonprofit organizations, and academic institutions are also exploring ways to use big data to accomplish their goals and missions. The explosion of interest in this area has created tremendous opportunities for those who have the skills to derive meaning from mountains of information.

"If you can't get insights until you've analyzed your sales for a week or a month, then you've lost sales within that time."[3]

—Naveen Peddamail, Walmart senior statistical analyst

Obtaining useful information from big data is not as easy as it might seem. There are many sources of big data, and the analysis must be tailored to the characteristics of each source. Knowing how to extract meaning from big data is a skill that relatively few people possess. As a result, qualified big data analysts are in great demand. Rob Bearden, the chief executive officer of Hortonworks, a business computer software company based in Santa Clara, California, says there are far more job openings than there are qualified people to fill them. "It's probably the biggest imbalance of supply and demand that I've ever seen in my career,"[4] he says.

What Does a Big Data Analyst Do?

Big data analysts use computer programs to extract meaningful information from vast amounts of rapidly changing digital data. This data often originates from a variety of sources, including social media platforms like Facebook, Twitter, and Instagram; online surveys and forms; and even queries of search engines like Google, Yahoo, and Bing. Online content, especially social media posts, can come in many different forms—not just words but also likes, emojis, maps, GPS readings, pictures, and videos. It also can be posted in a variety of formats, from short social media comments to long blog posts. Because big data is not organized into specific categories or consistent formats, it is referred to as unstructured data.

Traditional Data Analytics

Using computers to analyze large amounts of data is not new. Data analytics has been around for decades, but most data analysts worked with structured data. Structured data is information that has been organized and formatted into consistent categories. A Microsoft Excel spreadsheet is an example of structured data. Each computerized record is represented on a horizontal line on the spreadsheet. Parts of each record are placed in fields, or cells, on that line. These cells are aligned with other cells above and below them in vertical columns. The cells in the vertical column all belong in the same category. For example, the spreadsheet might arrange customer information with separate columns for first name, last name, street address, city, state, zip code. Data structured in this way is easy for a computer to work with because the data is all formatted in the same way and the categories do not change. For example, since every computer record in the example above has a cell in the zip code column, the data analyst might sort the customer records by zip code rather than by first or last name. The data analyst could then use the software program to add up the number of computer records, or customers, in each zip code or in a group of zip codes. This information would be useful to a marketing executive who needs to decide which zip code areas to advertise in.

Trained professionals known as data entry specialists are responsible for placing much structured data into specific fields of computer records. Other information is added by people when they complete online forms or surveys. For example, someone who is setting up an iTunes or Amazon customer account will create his or her own computer record when entering personal

Using Big Data to Monitor a Product Launch

In February 2014, Barclays, a multinational banking and financial services company based in London, launched Pingit. This smartphone app lets the bank's customers send money to other people using just their smartphone number. The new app became a social media sensation, which Barclays learned about, in part, because it used the big data analytics firm Sentiment Metrics to monitor social media reactions to the company and its products. Real-time reporting from Sentiment Metrics showed that positive reactions to Pingit far outnumbered negative comments.

However, Barclays executives were curious about the negative comments. Using the big data analytics, they found that a common complaint about the app was that people under age eighteen could not use it. This disappointed not only young people but also their parents, who were unable to transfer funds to their children. Within a week, Barclays had revamped the product so it could be used by sixteen- and seventeen-year-olds, avoiding a public relations disaster and showing its customers that it was responsive to their needs.

information into specific fields. There might be separate fields for the customer's name, address, phone number, credit card number, and e-mail address. These fields correspond to specific areas in the records. People might make mistakes when they enter data, of course, but such problems are easy to find and fix. For example, when someone is completing an online form, a software program often notifies the person if he or she has put incomplete or incorrect information in a field. This keeps the database from becoming cluttered with useless data.

The US census is an example of a structured database. Population surveys are mailed to all known US addresses and are also conducted by census takers who go door to door. The people who complete the surveys put data about themselves into specific fields. One field is for the number of people who live in the home. Other fields are for the names, ages, races, and occupations of the people living there. That data is placed into specific fields in the computer records. Once the census is complete, the data does not change. Although the number of census records is vast—more than 230 million of them—the data is highly structured and static (unchanging). As a result, it is easy for data analysts to use. They are able to use traditional software to sort the data in many ways and to create meaningful reports.

The Characteristics of Big Data

Big data is completely different from traditional, structured data. It is unstructured and constantly changing. In fact, some experts define big data by characteristics known as the four V's: volume, velocity, variety, and veracity.

Volume relates to the number of data records being analyzed. Big data gets its name from its volume, or size, which is extremely large. For example, the US census contains records for more than 230 million people. By contrast, Twitter produces twice that number of records each day—500 million tweets every twenty-four hours. An analysis of just five days' worth of tweets would involve 2.5 billion records, and an analysis of one year's worth of tweets would include more than 180 billion records. This is far more information than can be analyzed using traditional methods.

Big data is also generated at high speed, or velocity. For example, according to the Internet market research firm Brandwatch, Facebook's 1 billion daily users generate 4 million likes every minute, or 5.8 billion likes a day. They also post about 350 million photographs per day, which receive not only millions of likes but also millions of text comments. Similarly, Instagram users upload an average of 487 pictures every second, or more than 42 million photos a day. Traditional data processing methods cannot make sense of such rapidly changing data. "You're going from managing mildly complex data sets and volumes that are very structured [today] to sort of the Wild West of data," says Rob Bearden of Hortonworks. "It's high velocity. The volume is extraordinary."[5]

> "You're going from managing mildly complex data sets and volumes that are very structured [today] to sort of the Wild West of data."[5]
>
> —Rob Bearden, chief executive officer of Hortonworks

Big Data Analysts Correctly Predicted the Outcome of the 2016 Election

In the days before the 2016 US presidential election, nearly every traditional poll showed Hillary Clinton with a huge lead over Donald Trump. In fact, three days before the election the *New York Times* election forecast gave Clinton an 84 percent chance of winning. But across the Atlantic, Tom Jackson and Martin Sykora, big data analysts at Loughborough University in the United Kingdom, disagreed. "In the three weeks ahead of November 8, our model was telling us Trump was ahead based on the measures we were using," says Sykora.

Jackson and Sykora's big data platform, which they call Emotive, analyzed thousands of Twitter posts every second to understand how people felt about the two candidates. Using a methodology known as sentiment analysis, the Emotive algorithm placed the tweets into one of eight categories: anger, disgust, fear, happiness, sadness, surprise, shame, or confusion. The basic rule of the analysis was that the more tweets about a candidate that expressed extreme emotion, the fewer votes that candidate would receive. Emotive found that more people registered fear and anger about Trump than Clinton, but even larger numbers expressed more shame, sadness, surprise, and disgust about Clinton than Trump. Clinton's negatives translated into a narrow defeat in key states, and Trump won the election.

Quoted in Liam Quinn, "Two Academics Reveal How Twitter Told Them Donald Trump 'Dominated' the Campaign and Was a Lock to Beat Hillary," *Daily Mail*, December 25, 2016. www.dailymail.co.uk.

Variety is another trait of big data. Not only does big data include many different types of data—text, pictures, video—but it also can be posted in a variety of formats, from short social media comments to long blog posts. It is the unstructured nature of big data that presents the greatest challenge to data analysts trying to make sense of it. They must develop algorithms, or sets of computer rules, that will transform this raw, unstructured information into structured data for analysis. This process is known as normalization.

The fourth characteristic of big data is veracity, or truthfulness. Since big data often comes from the Internet, especially from social media, its accuracy has not been verified. The account it comes from might be fake; the statements might be untrue; the opinions might be artificial. For example, some companies and political campaigns pay people to post opinions that are not their own. This process is known as astroturfing, suggesting it represents something artificial as opposed to genuine grassroots popularity. Astroturfing and other misleading information can lead to faulty data analysis and cause those interested in the data to draw false conclusions. Data analysts must therefore find ways to cleanse big data of misleading data—a process known as scrubbing.

These factors mean that big data presents a range of new challenges to data analysts. As a result, many specialize in one aspect of big data rather than attempting to become an expert in all of it. Some analysts are known as technologists or data scientists. They write the algorithms and code that is used to organize and understand the large amounts of data. Other data analysts are known as quantification experts. They use statistics to reveal numerical patterns within the data. Some data analysts are sometimes called artist-explorers. They use algorithms to comb through the information to find something others have not seen.

Teaching Computers to Understand Language

A great deal of big data consists of words. This includes much of the data generated by Instagram and Facebook comments, tweets, and blog posts. When they write such content, Internet users often express themselves in casual language, using slang, abbreviations, and even misspellings. This kind of language is considered natural; that is, it is not structured for a machine to understand. "Unstructured big data is the things that humans are saying," says Tony Jewitt, vice president of Avalon Consulting, an information technology and services company in Plano, Texas. "It uses natural language."[6] To make sense of the written content in big data, analysts write algorithms that allow computers to find meaning in natural language. This process is known as natural language processing (NLP).

To a computer, words posted online are just strings of digits—the zeros and ones that make up binary code. These digits are devoid of meaning until the computer is given, or programmed with, a dictionary. The dictionary matches certain strings of binary code—the letters that make up a word—with other strings of code for the letters and words that define that word. Even then, a single word can mean many things to a human being, depending on how the word is used. For example, the word *file* can refer to a collection of data records in a computer, a tool used to smooth surfaces, or even a line of squares on a chessboard.

> "Unstructured big data is the things that humans are saying. It uses natural language."[6]
>
> —Tony Jewitt, vice president of Avalon Consulting

In addition, the meaning of a sentence in English depends on the order of the words, or syntax. "The girl ate the sandwich" means something very different from "The sandwich ate the girl," even though both sentences use the same words. To process language, computers must be taught rules of syntax for deciding on what strings of words mean. "Machines are still a long way from understanding everyday speech the way the computer Hal does in the motion picture *2001: A Space Odyssey*,"[7] says Preslav Nakov, a senior scientist at Qatar Computing Research Institute. The data scientist's algorithm must "teach" these different rules and meanings to the computer. This process is known as machine learning.

NLP and machine learning are two important tools that big data analysts use to make sense of big data. The big data analyst's toolkit also includes sentiment analysis—a method of detecting and quantifying the emotional qualities of big data—and statistical modeling to see how many times certain words are used in combination with other words. Those who have mastered these and other data analysis techniques have a bright future. "Data and big data analytics are becoming the life's blood of business," writes Thor Olavsrud, a senior writer for the technology website CIO. "Data scientists and data analysts as well as engineers and developers with the skills to work with big data technologies are sought after and well-compensated."[8]

CHAPTER 2

How Do You Become a Big Data Analyst?

Big data analysts must have a deep understanding of computer science, but they often combine their computing knowledge with concepts and principles from other disciplines to make sense of the data. All data analysts, but particularly quantification experts, need a strong background in statistics. Those working as artist-explorers often have formal training in marketing. Data analysts who work in a specialized field, such as health care, financial services, or science, often need education or experience relevant to that particular industry.

High School Preparation

Since big data is produced by computers, it does not exist apart from them. Therefore, it is essential for a big data analyst to have a solid knowledge of computer science. Students interested in becoming big data analysts need to understand not only the principles of software and databases but also the basics of computer hardware and networking, which make it possible to collect and analyze big data. "A background in computer science is very important," says Sriram Mohan, a professor of computer science at Rose-Hulman Institute of Technology in Terre Haute, Indiana. "You need the ability to program and also to think logically."[9]

The aspiring data analyst also needs a solid grasp of mathematics. Computer science and mathematics are closely related. Algorithms were developed in mathematics long before the invention of the modern computer, and computers themselves originated as mathematical calculating machines. At the simplest level, computers perform complex operations by mathematically manipulating strings of binary numbers. "Computer science is, in its most basic terms, nothing but binary mathematics,"[10] says

Harisha Manchale, a technologist at Tata Elxsi, an engineering firm in Bengaluru, India.

High school mathematics courses such as algebra, geometry, and calculus train students how to use logical procedures and abstract symbols to solve complex problems. "Abstract programming languages are very similar to the mathematical language that students learn in math class," says Lincoln Sedlacek, a communications specialist with Reasoning Mind, a nonprofit organization dedicated to helping provide high-quality math education for students. "From simple equalities to complex mathematical representations, learning mathematics teaches students the art of reading, comprehending, formulating thoughts, and communicating with abstract language."[11]

"A background in computer science is very important. You need the ability to program and also to think logically."[9]

—Sriram Mohan, a professor of computer science at Rose-Hulman Institute of Technology

Scientific principles are also valuable for big data analysts. High school chemistry, biology, and physics teach the kind of logic, reasoning, and methods that big data analysts employ in their work. Scientific subject matter also can be important if the big data analyst chooses to specialize in one of the sciences that employs big data, such as biology, astronomy, or physics. "Particle physics has been dealing with big data since its inception," says Robert Roser, head of the scientific computing division at the Fermi National Accelerator Laboratory (Fermilab) in Batavia, Illinois. "Big data is underlying all that we do."[12]

College Preparation

Big data analysts need to have at least a bachelor's degree in computer science or mathematics. Undergraduate coursework will include core mathematics not taken in high school, especially calculus, applied statistics, and linear and multilinear algebra. "Having a firm grasp of mathematics and science will help if the student wants to pursue a degree," says Chris Martino of the SimpliVity Corporation. "Most CS [computer science] programs are heavy in these areas with requirements in calculus, statistics, physics, etc."[13]

Undergraduate Coursework in Business Data Analytics

The W.P. Carey School of Business at Arizona State University in Tempe offers a bachelor's degree in business data analytics. It takes students eight terms to complete the degree, during which time they take more than thirty courses. Among them are the following:

- Computer Applications and Information Technology
- Brief Calculus
- Mathematics for Business Analysis
- Business Statistics
- Introduction to Business Data Analytics
- Business Writing
- Business Data Warehouses and Dimensional Modeling
- Fundamentals of Finance
- Marketing and Business Performance
- Business Data Mining
- Big Data Analytics and Visualization in Business
- Business Law and Ethics for Managers
- Enterprise Analytics
- Upper Division Business Data Analytics Elective

Arizona State University, "Business Data Analytics, BS." www.asu.edu.

Students interested in big data will benefit from focusing on data analytics at the college level. Data analytics includes the study of databases—how they are structured and how to extract data from them. Students who study data analytics learn computer languages such as SQL (Structured Query Language), which is used to manage relational databases, which contain highly structured data formatted in tables and rows. They also study NoSQL, which is used to manage non-relational databases, which contain unstructured data organized in groups or clusters.

Many also learn SAS (Statistical Analysis System), which is used to statistically analyze data. Computer science majors also learn about data integration, which involves merging data from one data management system to another or from a variety of sources into a single repository (known as a data warehouse). Data analytics students also learn sophisticated ways to identify patterns within large amounts of data, a process known as data mining.

Volunteer Opportunities and Internships

Gaining hands-on, practical experience is an important part of studying any science, including computer science. Many high schools have math clubs and computer clubs that offer a chance for students to meet professionals and visit laboratories. Because of the growing importance of big data, many private companies offer internships to students who are interested in working with big data. Some of the companies that hosted big data internships in 2016 included AT&T, Ralston Purina, and Samsung. Many colleges and universities, such as Brown University, Duke University, and the University of Washington, also advertised for big data interns to work in their computer labs.

Graduate Studies

Data scientists are highly educated. According to Burtch Works, an executive recruiting firm headquartered in Evanston, Illinois, more than nine out of ten data scientists (92 percent) have an advanced degree: 44 percent hold a master's degree, and 48 percent hold a doctorate. The most common fields of graduate study are mathematics and statistics (28 percent), followed by engineering (18 percent), computer science (17 percent), and natural science (16 percent).

Data analysts who have bachelor degrees can enter the field of big data analysis, but those who pursue graduate studies can learn and apply advanced computing concepts to big data. Graduate students study areas such as machine learning, natural language processing, computational linguistics, and artificial intelligence. Graduate students not only learn the theories that underlie these topics but also must devise software programs or data analytics models that actually work.

In 2013 New York University (NYU) became the first American graduate school to offer a master's degree focused on big data. "A new discipline has emerged to address the need for professionals and researchers to deal with the 'data tidal wave,'" states the NYU website. "Its object is to provide the underlying theory and methods of the data revolution. This emergent discipline is known by several names. We call it 'data science,' and we have created the world's first and only MS [master of science] degree program devoted to it."[14] The program requires students to complete thirty-six credits, half of which are required courses and half of which are electives. The program normally takes two years to complete. The degree culminates in a project that requires students to apply their theoretical knowledge to realistic settings, from collecting and processing real-world data to designing the best method to solve the problem.

> "If you're looking for a way to get an edge—whether you're job hunting, angling for a promotion or just want tangible, third-party proof of your skills—big data certification is a great option."[17]
>
> —Thor Olavsrud, a senior writer for CIO

Big data analysts are not required to have a doctorate, but those who do typically earn more and are able to find jobs faster. Several graduate schools in the United States now offer doctoral programs that are centered on big data. These include the Tandon School of Engineering at NYU, which offers a doctorate in computer science with specialization in visualization, databases, and big data; the University of Washington, Seattle, which offers a doctorate in big data and data science; and Colorado Technical University in Colorado Springs, Colorado, which offers a doctor of computer science degree with a concentration in big data analytics. Most of these programs take three to four years to complete. They typically require a student to take a range of courses that include machine learning, natural language processing, and sentiment analysis. Students also must demonstrate a depth of knowledge in a particular area by writing a dissertation—an in-depth paper based on their individual research and presenting an oral defense in which they answer questions about their work.

Certification and Licensing

Big data analysts need not be licensed to do their work. Formal certification is not required either, but it can help job candidates stand out from the crowd. This is especially true in a new field like big data. Job seekers hoping to land high-paying positions often claim to have experience with big data processing platforms such as Apache Hadoop, but in reality they do not. "People are slapping buzzwords on résumés and looking to get 50 or 100 percent more [pay], and they're getting it," says Scott Gnau, president of Teradata Labs. "There are a lot of folks who can spell Hadoop and put it on their résumé and call themselves data scientists, and nothing can be further from the truth."[15] Getting certified in Hadoop or another platform can remove all doubt about a candidate's ability to work with big data.

Certification is available from computing companies, nonprofit organizations, and institutions of higher learning. For example, the nonprofit INFORMS Computing Society, the largest professional society in the world for people who work in the fields of analytics, operations research, and management science, offers a program to become a certified analytics professional. The program certifies that those who complete the program have an end-to-end understanding of the analytics process. Similarly, Columbia University offers the Certification of Professional Achievement in Data Sciences program, which consists of four courses: Algorithms for Data Science, Probability and Statistics, Machine Learning for Data Science, and Exploratory Data Analysis and Visualization. Stanford University offers the Mining Massive Data Sets graduate certificate that requires candidates to demonstrate "mastery of efficient, powerful techniques and algorithms for extracting information from large datasets like the Web, social network graphs and large document repositories."[16] Companies such as IBM, Dell EMC, Revolution Analytics, and Cloudera also offer certification for professionals who work with their big data tools. "Data scientists and analysts with expertise in the techniques required to analyze big data . . . are hard to come by," writes Thor Olavsrud. "If you're looking for a way to get an edge—whether you're job hunting, angling for a promotion or just want tangible, third-party proof of your skills—big data certification is a great option."[17]

CHAPTER 3

What Skills and Personal Qualities Are Important to a Big Data Analyst?

Big data analysts combine strong technical skills with a certain amount of creativity. This helps them discover patterns and trends in computer activity that provide insights about what people are doing and thinking. In this way, big data analysis is both a science and an art. Although technical skills are required, it can be extremely helpful to have a working knowledge of business, marketing, and even psychology. "Too often, we focus too much on pure engineering/math ability, kicking business smarts to the wayside," says Frank Lo, the head of data science at DraftKings, a fantasy sports contest provider. "Data scientists create value by being consultants to the business."[18]

A Talent for Analysis

Long before they start crunching numbers, big data analysts must have a clear idea of what they are looking for. In biology, for example, the big data analyst must understand the scientist's hypothesis about what is causing a disease, condition, or biological behavior. For example, the scientist might believe there is a chemical reaction occurring at the molecular level that is affecting the way certain cells function. The big data analyst must then consider how to search for evidence of this reaction within the masses of data generated by machines that perform the biological experiments. Only after properly analyzing the problem can the analyst use software or original algorithms to tell the computer to look for the solution.

A Florida resident loads up on water and other essentials before a hurricane. When analysts for the Walmart chain evaluated buying patterns during hurricanes and other severe storms, they saw an increase in certain purchases and ordered more of those items ahead of the next storm.

Analytical skills are just as important once the analyst begins processing the data. The first time a data analyst uses a new algorithm or software program to extract information from big data, the process sometimes fails to produce the expected results. The data analyst must be able to look at the results, understand what went wrong, and know how to tweak the software to better extract meaning from the data. Big data analysts with a background in software engineering, systems engineering, or electrical engineering often excel at this kind of analysis. "We look for people with engineering backgrounds, because they think a certain way," says Tony Jewitt of Avalon Consulting. "They know how to break down a problem."[19]

In both the implementation of the analysis and its refinement, the data analyst must be very detail oriented. Even a tiny error in the software code can make a huge difference in the end result. This is especially true because of the enormity of the data sets. The sheer size of big data makes it extremely important to be accurate. A coding or querying error can skew the output and cause those involved in a project to make false conclusions. Errors can also increase the time it takes for the computer to complete the analysis. Even if results are accurate, they can lose their value if they take too long to process. For example, as Hurricane Sandy approached the United States in 2012, data analysts at Walmart studied buying patterns during previous hurricanes and severe storms. They found an upsurge in purchases of flashlights, batteries, and emergency equipment, as would be expected, but also of strawberry Pop-Tarts. Walmart executives ordered extra supplies of the breakfast pastries—which can be eaten without being heated—to stores in Hurricane Sandy's path, and they sold extremely well. If the analytics had taken days or even overnight to process, it would have been too late take action.

"The spirit of data science is discovery. Given a mountain of data, what inferences can we make? What truth is revealed or predicted? The strongest data scientists are motivated by this curiosity to explore data in very creative ways."[20]

—Frank Lo, head of data science at DraftKings

A Spirit of Inquiry

Big data analysts also need critical-thinking skills. These include the ability to think logically about the attributes of the big data, such as its variety (whether it is text only or text and pictures), the speed of its creation, whether it can be sorted by geographical location, the gender of its creators, and other variables. Critical thinking also involves a willingness to challenge assumptions and look at problems in a fresh way. "The spirit of data science is discovery," says Lo. "Given a mountain of data, what inferences can we make? What truth is revealed or predicted? The strongest data scientists are motivated by this curiosity to explore data in

Computational Thinking

In her groundbreaking 2006 essay, Jeannette Wing, the head of the Computer Science Department at Carnegie Mellon University in Pittsburgh, suggests that students learn to think about problems using methods employed by computer scientists, a process she calls computational thinking.

> Computational thinking is a fundamental skill for everyone, not just for computer scientists. To reading, writing, and arithmetic, we should add computational thinking to every child's analytical ability. . . .

> Computational thinking involves solving problems, designing systems, and understanding human behavior, by drawing on the concepts fundamental to computer science. . . .

> Consider these everyday examples: . . . At what point do you stop renting skis and buy yourself a pair?; that's online algorithms. Which line do you stand in at the supermarket?; that's performance modeling for multi-server systems. Why does your telephone still work during a power outage?; that's independence of failure and redundancy in design. . . .

> Thinking like a computer scientist means more than being able to program a computer. It requires thinking at multiple levels of abstraction. . . . Computational thinking is a way humans solve problems.

Jeannette M. Wing, "Computational Thinking," *Communications of the ACM*, March 2006. www.cs.cmu.edu.

very creative ways." This is why when Lo looks for analysts to join his work teams, he looks for people who not only excel at answering questions but also ask their own. "This genuine inquisitiveness is rocket fuel in driving a data scientist's search for meaningful discoveries in data."[20]

A data analyst must also possess a spirit of inquiry if he or she is to keep up with the rapidly changing industry. "A very important skill is the ability to learn new things, because the technology is always changing," says Professor Sriram Mohan. "Big data is not static."[21] In fact, some employers are less concerned with what job candidates already know than with their capacity to acquire new knowledge and skills. "What we hire for is the ability to learn," says Rachel Reinitz, a computer engineer with IBM. "The technology changes so fast."[22]

Many big data analysts take classes to get certified in new software and analysis tools. Others are more self-educated and keep their skills sharp by attending conferences, reading books, and watching videos produced by experts in the field. "I spend a lot of time reading books and blogs to try and keep up with new developments," says Mohan. "There are a lot of supportive communities online."[23]

> "What we hire for is the ability to learn. The technology changes so fast."[22]
>
> —Rachel Reinitz, a computer engineer with IBM

Math and Science

Although big data analysts must be inquisitive and creative, their problem-solving process often involves applying a new mathematical formula to their algorithm. This requires an understanding of high-level mathematics, such as multivariable calculus, linear and matrix algebra, or probability and statistics. "Numerical and statistical analysis are core quantitative skills that every good big data analyst needs,"[24] states Jigsaw Academy, an online education provider.

Big data analysts who work in scientific fields also need a strong background in the science they are investigating. In fact, some experts believe the scientific knowledge is more important than the computing skills. Robert Roser at Fermilab prefers to hire data analysts who have a background in particle physics. "Understanding the basics is most important,"[25] says Roser. The same is true for biology, astronomy, geophysics, or any of the scientific fields that need to analyze big data. A data analyst who does not have a scientific background will have a hard time asking the right questions to extract new and valuable information from the data. However, a scientist who has a deep understanding of

Big Data's Big Numbers

Big data analysts often use unusual numbers to describe quantities of data. For example, IBM states that "every day, we create 2.5 quintillion bytes of data." But what is a quintillion? That depends on where you are. In the United States, English-speaking Canada, and Australia, a quintillion is written as a one followed by eighteen zeros: 1,000,000,000,000,000,000. It can also be expressed as 10^{18}. In much of the rest of the world, a quintillion is a one followed by thirty zeros: 1,000,000,000,000,000,000,000, 000,000,000, or 10^{30}.

In the United States, each large number is one thousand times larger than the large number before it: a billion is one thousand times larger than a million; a trillion is one thousand times larger than a billion, and so on through quadrillion, quintillion, and sextillion.

In computing, a single binary digit (1 or 0) is called a bit. A byte is eight times larger than a bit. The numbers increase by a factor of 1,024 thereafter, so a kilobyte contains more than 1,000 bytes; a megabyte contains more than 1 million bytes; a gigabyte contains more than 1 billion bytes; a terabyte contains more than 1 trillion bytes; a petabyte contains more than 1 quadrillion bytes; an exabyte contains more than 1 quintillion bytes; and a zettabyte contains more than 1 sextillion bytes.

Kilobyte (KB)	1,024 Bytes
Megabyte (MB)	1,024 Kilobytes
Gigabyte (GB)	1,024 Megabytes
Terabyte (TB)	1,024 Gigabytes
Petabyte (PB)	1,024 Terabytes
Exabyte (EB)	1,024 Petabytes
Zettabyte (ZB)	1,024 Exabytes

For comparison, many laptop computers contain 1 terabyte of storage. Therefore, one exabyte is equal to the storage capacity of 1 million laptop computers, and one zettabyte is equal to the storage capacity of 1 billion laptops.

Quoted in IBM, "What Is Big Data?" www-01.ibm.com.

the subject matter can learn to use an existing big data tool or data analytics processing platform to ask meaningful questions about the data.

Teamwork and Communication

Analyzing big data involves using a variety of highly specialized skills, and it is rare for one person to excel at or even possess all of them. As a result, big data analysis is often conducted by several specialists who work together. An artist-explorer might set a direction for the project. A data analytics expert might organize the data. A software engineer might write the code that extracts the information. A data scientist might use machine learning or natural language processing to automate the data mining tasks, and a data mapper might create visualizations of the output. "No one person can do all that analysis," says Jewitt. Using a sports metaphor, Jewitt adds, "It takes a baseball team."[26]

Just as baseball players make adjustments and solve problems by communicating with each other in the field, so too must big data analysts be able to share their ideas and coordinate with other members of their team. Because big data analysis is a highly technical field, data scientists sometimes find it challenging to describe their work to team members and executives who are not as technologically savvy as they are. "We need workers who can communicate with others who have nontechnical backgrounds,"[27] explains Jewitt. Similarly, marketing experts can have trouble translating their wants and needs into a language the technologists understand. To be effective, a data analyst must therefore be both a good listener and a clear speaker. "At a later stage of a project, we meet with customers to find out what they think about the results they are getting with the tools we designed," says Mina Farid, a data scientist at Thomson Reuters Labs in Ontario, Canada. "We employ this feedback to modify the tool being built. This communication is extremely helpful, and it continues until we meet the [customer's] expectations."[28]

CHAPTER 4

What Is It Like to Work as a Big Data Analyst?

Big data analysis is now being undertaken in many different industries. According to the Bureau of Labor Statistics (BLS), big data analysts are concentrated in six sectors: government, business, financial institutions, health care, scientific research facilities, and colleges and universities. A big data analyst's pay, working conditions, and educational requirements can vary from one industry to another.

Big Data Analytics in Government

The largest percentage of big data analysts—15 percent—work within the government. A large number work in the field of intelligence. Since the terrorist attacks of September 11, 2001, the workforce of the National Security Agency (NSA), the nation's intelligence-gathering agency, has grown from twenty-two thousand to thirty-three thousand. In addition, the *Washington Post* reports that the number of private companies working with the NSA has more than tripled, from 150 to close to 500. Together these companies analyze huge amounts of unstructured data with the goal of preventing a terrorist attack.

Much of the NSA's data is gathered by seven Advanced Orion spy satellites, each of which is equipped with a mesh antenna the size of a football field. These satellites intercept millions of text, voice, image, and other communications from cell phones and other electronic devices each day. This high volume of unstructured data is sent to the processing centers on the ground, where big data analysts work with it in real time. "The foreign signals that NSA collects are invaluable to national security," the agency said in a statement released in 2013. "This information helps the agency determine where adversaries are located, what they're

Health department data analysts assess Zika-related statistics and other information to determine how and where the mosquito-borne virus is spreading. Their work helps officials respond quickly to public health threats like this.

planning, when they're planning to carry it out, with whom they're working, and the kinds of weapons they're using."[29]

The government analyzes big data for areas other than defense, too. Big data analysts work in health-related research, energy exploration, financial market analysis, fraud detection, and to protect the environment. For example, data analysts at the Department of Health and Human Services use big data to track the spread of contagious diseases and food-borne illnesses. The analysis helps public health officials to respond quickly to health threats, provide faster treatment, and save lives. "Big Data will let us watch flu outbreaks bloom and direct scarce vaccines to the most critical areas," writes venture capitalist Michael Harden. "We can catch . . . outbreaks [of disease] before they spread and days before any savvy doc manages to call in to alert the CDC [Centers for Disease Control and Prevention]."[30]

The Social Security Administration (SSA) is another government agency that uses big data analytics. The SSA must evaluate disability and retirement claims that arrive in the form of unstructured data. Analytics help the agency process claims more quickly while also detecting suspicious or fraudulent claims. Meanwhile, the Security and Exchange Commission, which regulates the trading of stocks and other financial instruments, uses big data analytics to monitor financial market activity. It has begun to use network analytics and natural language processing to identify illegal trading activity.

Big Data in the Financial Industry

Millions of electronic financial transactions take place every day across a range of devices—ATMs, point-of-sale machines, smartphones, and computers. Visa Inc., a financial services company, processes more than 172 million credit and bank card transactions a day. These transactions generate massive amounts of data. This data must be integrated in real time with other information, such as customer account details and their bank balances. It also must be preserved so it can be reviewed, or audited, later. In addition, financial institutions must be constantly on alert against the illegal use of bank cards and credit cards, money laundering, and identity theft, which is when a person illegally obtains and uses a customer's account information to defraud the institution out of funds. All of these activities generate big data.

In addition to customer-generated big data, financial institutions also must manage big data that pertains to investments. This includes making financial trades at high velocity, archiving it, and detecting fraud. Banks, stock brokerages, hedge funds, and other organizations involved in the financial markets use big data to analyze investor sentiments, predict market trends, and plan trades. "Lurking deep within the petabyte-sized pools of market data around the world are patterns and customer insights that can mean the difference between index-topping ideas and average numbers,"[31] states the Teradata website.

Big Data and Health Care

Numerous lab tests and large amounts of patient information mean that the health care sector generates huge amounts of electronic data. However, few in the industry have been able to use

A Day in the Life of a Big Data Analyst

Scott Kamino is a big data analyst for Inflection, a company that creates background reports. He describes his typical day:

> 8:00 a.m.—. . . I log into my computer, check my list of tasks, and pick something challenging to take advantage of my refreshed mind. . . .
>
> 9:30 a.m.—I head to morning scrum [meeting] with the People-Smart [client] team. I use this as an opportunity to hear what everyone's working on and stay connected to the product vision. . . .
>
> 10:00 a.m.—I start working on a dashboard for a new PeopleSmart feature called SQUID—System for Quality User Informed Data. SQUID allows PeopleSmart users to provide feedback and flag incorrect information on reports. . . .
>
> 1:00 p.m.—I meet with James, one of our data engineers. . . . We talk about adding event tracking to . . . the website as well as creating a few tables to better measure customer engagement. . . .
>
> 2:00 p.m.—I get a ping from Josh, a PeopleSmart product manager. . . . He wants additional metrics to better gauge the tests. . . . I head back to my machine, log onto our SQL server, and pull some data on retention and repeat purchases. . . .
>
> 5:30 p.m.—The brain starts feeling a little scrambled so I head out.

Scott Kamino, "A Day in the Life of a Data Analyst: Scott Kamino," *Slope* (blog), Inflection, June 3, 2015. http://inflection.com.

that data to provide improved patient care and reduce expense because the vast majority of the information is unstructured. According to *Forbes*, 80 percent of medical and clinical information about patients consists of unstructured data, such as physician notes. "If we want to learn how to better care for individuals and understand more about the health of the population as a whole, we need to be able to mine unstructured data for insights,"[32] says Darren Schulte, the chief executive officer of Apixio, a company that specializes in analyzing big data. Health care executives are beginning to realize that big data analysis can provide a meaningful overview of what diseases are being actively treated, how severe they are, and what treatments are being used. Big data can also reveal gaps in care. For example, big data analysis can draw attention to situations where a physician noted a chronic disease in the patient history but has not provided a recent assessment.

> "These technologies will offer new opportunities to analyze big and fast data, see patterns, and make accurate predictions based on these patterns."[33]
>
> —Audie Hittle, chief technology officer at EMC Isilon

As a result of the promise of big data, a survey of 150 health care executives conducted by software giant Dell EMC and the government information technology networking group MeriTalk found that 59 percent of respondents said that in five years the successful use of big data would be vital to fulfilling their agency's objectives. "These technologies will offer new opportunities to analyze big and fast data, see patterns, and make accurate predictions based on these patterns," says Audie Hittle, the chief technology officer at EMC Isilon. "It will allow agencies to be more productive, and increase intelligence and agility."[33]

A few health care providers are already using big data to improve patient care. For example, big data analysts at Beth Israel Hospital use data collected from millions of patients through a smartphone app to help doctors make informed decisions about which drugs to prescribe. This eliminates the need to subject every patient to a battery of expensive lab tests.

Most of a big data analyst's daily tasks are similar, regardless of the industry. Data analysts meet with clients to find out what information they want to extract from the data. If the analyst works for a consulting firm, the client might be another company that does not have the ability to process big data. If the analyst works for a company that does process big data, the client might be an executive within the company who works for marketing or operations. In a scientific setting, the client might be a scientist in charge of an experiment. In each situation the big data analyst must listen carefully to what the client wants and then ask questions to probe deeper into their needs. Once data analytics begins, analysts will meet with the clients to present results and receive feedback on their work.

Among an analyst's most important responsibilities is to keep up to date on advances in the field. By reading about what others are doing, an analyst learns which techniques are yielding results

"14 Million Selfies" per Second

Scientific observations and experiments can generate enormous amounts of data. For example, the Large Hadron Collider (LHC) operated by the European Organization for Nuclear Research, known as CERN, smashes atomic and subatomic particles together at almost the speed of light, causing the particles to break into even smaller particles. To record these collisions, LHC sensors take 14 million readings per second. "It's akin to saving 14 million selfies with every tick of a watch's second hand," writes Lucas Mearian, a senior writer with *Computerworld*. The LHC sensors generate massive amounts of data—3 gigabytes of data per second, or about the amount of data the average smartphone customer uses in a month. That adds up to about 25 petabytes (25 million gigabytes) of data per year. "The amount of data produced at CERN was impressive ten years ago, but is not as impressive as what's produced today," says Guenther Dissertori, a professor of particle physics at CERN. Dissertori says the amount of data generated will grow immensely in the next ten to twenty years as the collider's power increases. "The electronics will be improved so we can write out more data packages per second than we do now."

Quoted in Lucas Mearian, "CERN's Data Stores Soar to 530M Gigabytes," *Computerworld*, August 14, 2015. www.computerworld.com.

(and which are not). The analyst might read scientific papers published in computer science journals, articles by renowned data scientists, or blog entries by teams within companies that provide big data solutions. Occasionally an analyst will take a training course or attend a conference to become more familiar with the latest technologies.

Most of an analyst's time is spent designing ways to extract meaningful information from the data. This work can be purely mental and may involve conceptualizing the approach. Or it can involve creating an algorithm or revising software that already exists. Once a working model of the program—known as a proof of concept—is functioning, the analyst will test it out on the data. This can involve many rounds of testing the algorithm, revising it, and testing it again.

The Working Environment

Big data analysts spend the majority of their time in their offices analyzing problems, designing solutions, and meeting clients or other team members. Data analysts who work for consulting firms will sometimes go off-site to meet with clients and discuss the project. The job can include some traveling, especially if the analyst attends conferences. Big data conferences are held all around the world. It would not be unusual for a big data analyst to travel abroad to exchange ideas with others in the field.

Big data analysts often work on projects where the client or the company is seeking information that will give it a competitive advantage. In these cases, the data analyst might be expected to work nights and weekends to meet deadlines. This is especially true during the testing phase, when the analyst is tasked with processing a live stream of data from a social media source such as Twitter, Instagram, or Facebook.

Big Salaries for Big Data

Because of the advanced education and unique skills they must possess, big data analysts earn well above the national average of all occupations. According to the BLS, in May 2015 the median annual wage for statisticians—a group that includes big data analysts—was $80,110. That figure is more than twice the median annual wage for all occupations ($36,200). The lowest 10 percent of big data analysts earned less than $44,900, and the highest 10 percent earned more than $130,630.

A survey conducted in April 2016 by the executive recruiting firm Burtch Works found the median annual wage for data scientists to be considerably higher than that of other data analytics positions. Burtch Works separates data scientists from other data analytics positions because of the nature of the data they analyze. "We distinguish between the two because data scientists, by our definition, manage unstructured data or continuously streaming data, using computer science skills that are uncommon for traditional predictive analytics professionals, who manage structured data," writes Linda Burtch, the firm's managing director. Burtch Works divides data scientists into three levels. Its survey found that level-one data scientists earn a median annual wage of $97,000; level-two data scientists earn a median annual wage of $125,000; and level-three data scientists earn a median annual wage of $152,000. In addition, Burtch Works found that "more than 73 percent of all data scientists are eligible for bonuses, and the median bonus they received range from $10,000 to $21,000."[34]

> "Data scientists, by our definition, manage unstructured data or continuously streaming data, using computer science skills that are uncommon for traditional predictive analytics professionals, who manage structured data."[34]
>
> —Linda Burtch, managing director of Burtch Works

Wages for big data analysts vary by industry. According to the BLS, statisticians and big data analysts who work for the federal government earn an annual wage of $99,300. Those in scientific research and development services earn $89,490 a year. Those who work in the fields of finance and insurance earn an annual wage of $79,190. Those in management, scientific, and technical consulting services earn $76,450 a year, and those in colleges, universities, and professional schools earn $68,970 a year.

CHAPTER 5

Advancement and Other Job Opportunities

People who have a working knowledge of big data can expect to be promoted into positions where they supervise the new data analysts flooding into the field. Career paths differ depending on the industry in which one works. The three major industries are business, government, and academia.

The Business Path

The career path for a big data analyst in the business sector is clearly defined. The new hire in this field is given the title of data analyst. After a period of time and demonstrated success with the platforms and the data unique to that company, the data analyst is promoted to senior data analyst. In this position he or she has increased responsibility and gets a pay raise but does not formally oversee other data analysts. The senior data analyst might become a team leader, if the company uses formal teams.

If the senior data analyst has developed innovative algorithms or software improvements, he or she might be promoted to analytics manager. The analytics manager oversees the technical progress made by various teams, hires new employees, and approves minor purchases of software and equipment that helps the team. According to a salary study by Burtch Works, analytics managers count as level-one data scientist managers, earning a median salary of $140,000 a year.

An especially capable analytics manager might move up to become director of analytics. This person ensures the quality and integrity of data analytics operations using standard industry techniques. He or she also supervises the work of many teams.

Using Big Data to Save Lives

When an earthquake measuring 7.8 on the Richter Scale struck the mountainous nation of Nepal on April 25, 2015, more than eight thousand people were killed and twenty-one thousand were injured. To find out where first responders were most needed, officials at the United Nations contacted Patrick Meier, a data scientist who maintains Artificial Intelligence for Disaster Response, a big data platform that collects, identifies, and classifies social media messages posted after a natural disaster. Based on the analysis of three hundred thousand tweets, Meier and his team plotted the locations of the most urgent tweets on so-called crisis maps.

Meier sent the maps to relief agencies so they could focus on the areas that required immediate attention. "Within 24 hours of the first tremors in Nepal . . . we had the opportunity to put together live crisis maps of the most affected areas and then feed these to several relief agencies before they had even arrived," said Meier. "This meant that responders had a good picture of the areas that had received the worst of the damage before they had even touched down in [the capital] Kathmandu."

Quoted in *Qatar Tribune*, "QCRI's Digital Initiatives Boost Nepal Earthquake Relief Works," May 26, 2015. www.qatar-tribune.com.

By knowing what approaches and techniques are working in various areas, directors of analytics are able to transfer knowledge and promote best practices. The director of analytics keeps upper management informed of the progress being made, setbacks that have occurred, and any needs the teams have. Directors of analytics might recommend large purchases that need to be made, such as hardware and software upgrades, but they might not have the authority to actually make the purchases. They also promote or recruit data analytics managers. According to Burtch Works, data analytics managers count as data scientist managers, earning a median salary of $190,000 a year.

The next rung on the corporate ladder is vice president of analytics. This person reports to the company president, the chief technology officer, or the chief information officer. He or she develops long-term strategies for the company and plans ways data analytics can help the organization achieve its goals. Vice presidents also promote or recruit directors of analytics and plan the growth of the analytics division. They work with the finance department to develop budgets and can usually approve major purchases. They sometimes meet directly with large vendors to negotiate contracts and deals. According to the Burtch Works survey, vice presidents count as level-three data science managers, earning a base salary between $226,250 and $277,750 a year, with the median annual wage being $240,000.

Big Data Analysts in Academia

Many big data analysts work in the computer science departments of colleges, universities, and government laboratories, where they conduct research. Usually this research tries to solve complex data analytics problems that are not being worked on

Big data analysts can help scientists understand the possible genetic connections to certain illnesses. In one study, scientists sought to learn why some patients with brain cancer died more quickly than others.

in the private sector, often because there is no clear application for their use or the solution would be too expensive to develop. However, these discoveries often are adopted by business and government once their value is proven.

Other academic research can involve fields outside computer science that make use of big data in observations or experiments. Scientists in the fields of biomedicine, physics, and astronomy all work with enormous data sets that require big data analysis. For example, scientists in the field of genomics work with data about the human genome, the chemical instruction set that tells the cells in the body how to grow and what to do. The human genome includes 3.3 billion chemical units. Genomic scientists use big data analytics to compare sections of the human genome taken from both healthy and diseased volunteers to see if they can identify genetic differences that cause a disease or affect its course.

In 2016 a team of scientists analyzed the genomic information of 1,122 patients with brain cancer to see if they could learn why some patients died from the disease quickly, but others survived for several years. The study identified groups of patients with similar genes that had similar outcomes. "This project is an example of the advantage of Big Data," says Michele Ceccarelli, a senior scientist at Hamad Bin Khalifa University in Doha, Qatar. "In order to make our discovery, we worked with a network of more than 300 scientists from around the world. We analyzed the millions of pieces of information that formed a 'data tsunami.'. . . As a result of our analysis we discovered two novel subgroups of patients that were previously unknown."[35]

Working at the cutting edge of computer science, big data analysts who work in a college or university setting usually are required to have a doctorate. The academic career path is clearly defined, but it is quite different from the career path in business.

> "This project is an example of the advantage of Big Data. In order to make our discovery, we worked with a network of more than 300 scientists from around the world. . . . We discovered two novel subgroups of patients that were previously unknown."[35]
>
> —Michele Ceccarelli, senior scientist at Hamad Bin Khalifa University

Whether a person advances is often determined by the number and quality of papers he or she publishes in peer-reviewed journals, whether they present at conferences, and whether they are granted any patents. Big data analysts or data scientists who pursue the academic track also have responsibilities to students. They might teach courses or serve as advisers. They also might be required to serve on academic committees or on the editorial boards of academic journals.

Big Data and Government

Big data analysts who work in government laboratories are often referred to as data scientists. The US government uses big data in many ways. The Department of Transportation uses big data to analyze video surveillance of people as they travel by car, train, and plane. Doing so helps it gain insights about where new infrastructure is needed. The CDC uses big data to track the spread of illness and post real-time data analysis on its FluView webpage. The Department of Agriculture uses planting and harvesting data from computerized farm equipment to learn how to increase crop yields. The analysts are able to create "prescriptions" right down to the individual acre based on soil, weather, and other conditions. "Today, with this technology, we have the ability to go into a field and break that field up into regions or zones and plant two different hybrids," says Scott Shearer, a professor at Ohio State University. "The analytics are going to drive the development of those prescriptions."[36]

> "Today, with this technology, we have the ability to go into a field and break that field up into regions or zones and plant two different hybrids."[36]
>
> —Scott Shearer, a professor at Ohio State University

Other Occupations

A career in big data analytics can open the door to other professions, too. A data scientist at a college or university might decide that the best part of the job is interacting with students. He or she might decide to pursue teaching full time. This might require going back to school to take education courses and earn a teaching credential.

Some successful big data analysts choose to offer their services as consultants, either by starting their own consultancy group or by signing on to another firm as a private contractor. Self-employed data analysts often enjoy having control over their work schedules, meeting new people, and working on different kinds of projects. Successful consultants are able to focus on their own research interests rather than the needs of one company or government department.

CHAPTER 6

What Does the Future Hold for Big Data Analysts?

In his June 2013 article about employment opportunities in the field of big data, CNBC reporter Chris Morris described the position of data analyst as "the Sexiest Job of the 21st Century." Morris explained that "with more and more companies using big data, the demand for data analytic specialists—sometimes called data scientists, who know how to manage the tsunami of information, spot patterns within it and draw conclusions and insights—is nearing a frenzy."[37] The research firm McKinsey reports that 140,000 to 190,000 people with big data analytic skills will be needed to fill jobs by 2018. There also is a shortage of marketing and business people who understand big data. McKinsey reports that an additional 1.5 million managers and analysts who understand how to use big data to make decisions will be needed by 2018. Rob Bearden of Hortonworks states that "the talent pool is, at best, probably 20 percent of the demand."[38]

The Number-One Job for Balancing Work and Life

The shortage of qualified big data analysts means that qualified professionals can earn big salaries. "Someone right out of school can earn $125,000, while someone with a year or two of experience and a demonstrated skill set can easily make double that,"[39] writes Morris. But companies are using more than salaries to attract qualified analysts, according to Stan Ahalt, director of the Renaissance Computing Institute at the University of North Carolina at Chapel Hill. "The demand for people who are able to analyze massive amounts of data and extract actionable decisions has really blossomed," says Ahalt. "The people who are being hired are being highly sought-after, so I suspect they're getting relatively good offers, and offers that include flexibility in their hours and locations simply because there are many more jobs than there are people."[40]

Because of the flexibility and other benefits that companies grant to big data analysts, *Forbes* magazine ranked data scientist at the top of its list of best jobs for work-life balance. "Much discussed and rarely achieved in full, work-life balance is an elusive prize in modern professional culture," wrote *Forbes* staffer Kathryn Dill. "While it can depend greatly on the priorities and values of an individual and their manager, some jobs provide strong opportunities for those looking to combine a fulfilling career with a thriving personal life. . . . Topping the list of jobs that provide strong work-life balance is data scientist."[41]

"With more and more companies using big data, the demand for data analytic specialists—sometimes called data scientists, who know how to manage the tsunami of information, spot patterns within it and draw conclusions and insights—is nearing a frenzy."[37]

—Chris Morris, reporter for CNBC

The BLS is a bit more conservative in its estimates of future employment prospects for statisticians and big data analysts. Even so, it still projects faster growth than in almost any other profession. The BLS estimates that employment of statisticians and big data analysts will grow 34 percent through 2024, or about five times faster than the average for all occupations. The BLS forecasts that the number of statistician and big data jobs will grow from 30,000 to 40,100 through 2024.

Behind the Growth in Big Data Jobs

Employment forecasters see two main reasons for the growth in big data jobs. One is the number of organizations that are adopting big data analytics as a way to understand the public and predict trends. According to the *Economist*, the data analytics industry is currently worth more than $100 billion and is growing at the rate of almost 10 percent a year, roughly twice as fast as the software business as a whole. In fact, the market is so promising that four companies—Oracle, IBM, Microsoft, and SAP—have spent more than $15 billion buying software firms that specialize in data management and analytics.

The other factor driving the growth of the profession is the mind-boggling expansion of big data itself. The *Economist* reports that Walmart's databases are estimated to contain more than 2.5 petabytes of data—the equivalent of 167 times the books in the Library of Congress. This is one reason why Rollin Ford, Walmart's chief information officer, is constantly looking for ways to improve his job and profession. "Every day I wake up and ask, 'how can I flow data better, manage data better, analyze data better?'"[42] he says.

> "Every day I wake up and ask, 'how can I flow data better, manage data better, analyze data better?'"[42]
>
> —Rollin Ford, chief information officer for Walmart

Walmart and other retailers are not the only ones contributing to the growth of big data. Internet activity also generates vast quantities of information. According to the software company Domo, every minute of every day, Google receives 2 million search queries, Apple receives 47,000 app downloads, brands and organizations receive 34,722 likes, and consumers spend $272,000 on web shopping. Each of these actions and transactions generate mountains of data that contain valuable information for those interested in looking for it.

Analyzing Data from the Internet of Things

Humans are not the only ones contributing to big data; machines are doing it too. Automated cameras, sensors, and other devices produce a constant stream of data. These interconnected devices are often referred to as the Internet of Things (IoT). According to Juniper Research, the total number of such devices currently stands at 13.4 billion and is expected to grow to 38.5 billion devices by 2020. Some of these devices are in the home;

The Astronomical Growth of Big Data

Sometime in the 2020s scientists will flip a switch and turn on the Square Kilometre Array (SKA). This is the world's largest radio telescope. It has some 2,000 high- and mid-frequency antennas and 1 million low-frequency antennas arrayed over a square kilometer of collecting area. The SKA will enable astronomers to survey the sky in greater detail and much faster than any system that currently exists. "The SKA will be able to conduct transformational science, breaking new ground in astronomical observations," says the SKA website, and "re-define our understanding of space as we know it." It also will generate more data than any machine in existence—an astounding 700 terabytes of data per second. The telescope will require big data analytics on a scale never seen before. Scientists, engineers, and big data analysts from one hundred organizations in twenty countries are currently designing and developing a system that includes supercomputers faster than any in existence and network technology that will generate more data traffic than the entire Internet does today.

Square Kilometre Array, "SKA Project." www.skatelescope.org.

these include smart televisions, security systems, and temperature control systems. Many more have been deployed in industrial settings and public service sectors to monitor water, oil, and gas pipelines; traffic; and electrical grids. IDC, a company that forecasts trends in the technology sector, estimates that by 2020 the IoT will generate 10 percent of the world's data, up from just 2 percent in 2014. The devices will produce 4.4 zettabytes of data—enough to fill a stack of iPads reaching two-thirds of the way to the moon. According to IDC's Digital Universe study, the total amount of data on the planet will double every two years through 2020. The production of new data is growing faster even than the ability to store it. In 2013 storage systems could hold 33 percent of all data. By 2020 they will be able to hold less than

Companies like Google and Apple have contributed to the explosive growth of big data. Google receives 2 million search queries every minute of every day, according to one software research company.

half that amount—only 15 percent. The rest of the data is simply erased to make room for new data. In the future, more big data analysts will be employed to extract useful information from the IoT before the data is destroyed.

Not only will the IoT generate more data overall, but IDC predicts that the IoT will increase the amount of so-called useful data in existence—that is, data that can be analyzed. In 2013 only 22 percent of the world's output of data was considered useful, and only a small portion of that—less than 5 percent—was actually analyzed. Because of the IoT, IDC estimates that 35 percent of all data could be considered useful by 2020. Vernon Turner, the senior vice president at IDC, believes more big data analysts will be needed to transform this useful data into assets for business. "As sensors become connected to the internet, the data they generate becomes increasingly important to every aspect of business, transforming old industries into new, relevant entities,"[43] says Turner. Maryanne Gaitho, a business insight and retail account manager for Nokia International, agrees. "Industry influencers, academicians, and other prominent stakeholders certainly agree that big data has become a big game changer in most, if not all, types of modern industries over the last few years," writes Gaitho. "As big data continues to permeate our day-to-day lives, there has been a significant shift of focus from the hype surrounding it to finding real value in its use."[44]

CHAPTER 7

Interview with a Big Data Analyst

Mina Farid is a data scientist at Thomson Reuters Labs in Waterloo, Ontario, Canada. He answered questions about his career by mail.

Q: Why did you become a big data analyst?

A: To me, technology has always been about helping people—for example, to make their lives better, provide more entertainment, or help them in their businesses. The role of a data scientist is to help customers unlock the value of their data. Everybody has data in their business, whether it is about retail, customers, blog posts, or interaction with customers over social media websites.

My favorite quote is what Sherlock Holmes says in *The Adventure of the Copper Beeches*: "Data! data! data!" he cried impatiently. "I can't make bricks without clay." Like Sherlock Holmes, data scientists explore large amounts of data to find relevant information that might be scattered across multiple data sets in different domains [areas of a company] and come up with high-level insights and conclusions or support a particular hypothesis. Businesses collect a lot of data, but they do not realize its potential. If analyzed correctly on time, data can provide deep insights to help business owners and decision makers.

Data science is an art! It is not just about knowing how to use some libraries, but more about using a palette of technical tools to draw conclusions from the underlying data.

Q: Can you describe your typical workday?

A: I typically do a few different things every day. We work on fast-paced sprints; therefore, there are many things that need to be done over the course of a single week. In the early stages of a project, there is a process of designing proposals that are relevant to a customer's needs. One important aspect of data science is to be sure that we are building something useful in the first place. Since all our work is supposed to provide insights or build tools to help someone in their job, we must make sure we are producing a valuable output and that there is a customer need for it.

I spend the majority of the day analyzing data using algorithms that I develop to solve a particular problem with the help of known statistical tools and libraries. Therefore, it is important to know how to code in order to build a proof of concept of the ideas we are building or to produce results of an analysis that supports or contradicts a hypothesis. Occasionally, I need to familiarize myself with new technologies that are relevant to a particular project.

Q: What do you like most about your job?

A: I love the fact that I work on many different projects in different domains. This is because the company I work at (Thomson Reuters) does business in many domains, e.g., finance and risk, legal, and taxes. Moreover, we do business with many other companies, such as consulting firms, banks, law firms, investment companies, and others. This exposure to multiple [industries] forces us to get familiar with many sectors and how they operate. This makes me a well-rounded person with knowledge about many fields.

Another thing that I enjoy is the flexibility of working hours and location, as creativity has no limitations of time or place. However, this flexibility is a double-edged sword; it can kill the work-life balance because I *could* be working at any point of time.

Q: What do you like least about your job?

A: A challenge that I usually face in this job is bias. It is very easy to interpret the results of an analysis as we want. In other words, if you keep listening to your data, it will eventually tell you what you want to hear. It is important to be open to the conclusion that the initial hypothesis is wrong (or that data does not support it). Another problem that is relevant to working at a big company is the number of meetings that we need to attend. Not all of them might be relevant to my work or expertise, so it might not be the best way to spend work hours.

Q: What personal qualities do you find most valuable for this type of work?

A: There are a few skills that a data scientist needs to possess. Sometimes, there are no specific requirements for a project. In such cases, the data scientist is responsible for determining the scope of the project—what it should include and what it should not include—by understanding the customer needs and exploring the available data. This requires good interpersonal skills to understand how people do their job, especially that we deal with customers from different sectors and domains. . . . Also, data scientists need to not be biased when they interview customers. During the interview, the data scientist must avoid leading customers into a specific direction, especially when they do not know what they are looking for.

Q: What advice do you have for students who might be interested in this career?

A: Study statistics and its applications in real life. Data science is a very dynamic field, but the foundation for understanding data is not going to change; it is all based on statistics, especially at an era of big data. You also need to stay up to date with the latest technologies in data management—for example, search engines, database management systems, and other machine learning and artificial intelligence tools in general. The first few months in the career are going to be a high learning curve unless you already possess solid understanding of the underlying models. Also, there are a lot of publicly available data sets and open-source tools. Go over the data and try to run different kinds of analysis. If possible, also try to join datathons [twenty-four-hour events in which teams of data analysts compete to solve complex problems using the same big data sets] to get a glimpse of what a small data science project looks like.

SOURCE NOTES

Introduction: Discovering Meaning in Digital Data

1. Quoted in Robin McKie, "Farewell, Rosetta: Space Mission to End on Collision Course with Comet," *Guardian*, September 11, 2016. www.theguardian.com.
2. John Gantz and David Reinsel, *The Digital Universe in 2020: Big Data, Bigger Digital Shadows, and Biggest Growth in the Far East*. Framingham, MA: IDC Go-to-Market Services, December 2012, p. 5.
3. Quoted in Bernard Marr, "The Most Practical Big Data Use Cases of 2016," *Forbes*, August 25, 2016. www.forbes.com.
4. Quoted in Chris Morris, "The Sexiest Job of the 21st Century: Data Analyst," CNBC, June 5, 2013. www.cnbc.com.

Chapter 1: What Does a Big Data Analyst Do?

5. Quoted in Morris, "The Sexiest Job of the 21st Century."
6. Quoted in Sara Royster, "Working with Big Data," *Occupational Outlook Quarterly*, Fall 2013, p. 3.
7. Preslav Nakov and Marti Hearst, "60 Years Ago People Dreamed of Talking with a Machine. Are We Any Closer?," paper presented at the Fourth Joint Conference on Lexical and Computational Semantics: *SEM, June 5, 2015.
8. Thor Olavsrud, "16 Big Data Certifications That Will Pay Off," CIO, July 31, 2014. www.cio.com.

Chapter 2: How Do You Become a Big Data Analyst?

9. Quoted in Royster, "Working with Big Data," p. 9.
10. Harisha Manchale, "How Is Mathematics Related to Computer Science?," Quora, March 13, 2013. www.quora.com.
11. Lincoln Sedlacek, "Math Education: The Roots of Computer Science," *STEM* (blog), Edutopia, April 20, 2016. www.edutopia.org.
12. Quoted in Royster, "Working with Big Data," pp. 6–7.
13. Quoted in Maggie O'Neill, "Computer Science Before College," Computer Science Online. www.computerscienceonline.org.

14. NYU Center for Data Science, "Master of Science in Data Science." http://cds.nyu.edu.

15. Quoted in Morris, "The Sexiest Job of the 21st Century."

16. Stanford University, "Mining Massive Data Sets Graduate Certificate." http://scpd.stanford.edu.

17. Olavsrud, "16 Big Data Certifications That Will Pay Off."

Chapter 3: What Skills and Personal Qualities Are Important to a Big Data Analyst?

18. Frank Lo, "Tips for Hiring Data Scientists from Frank Lo," *Burtch Works Blog*, March 12, 2014. www.burtchworks.com.

19. Quoted in Royster, "Working with Big Data," p. 9.

20. Lo, "Tips for Hiring Data Scientists from Frank Lo."

21. Quoted in Royster, "Working with Big Data," p. 9.

22. Quoted in Steve Lohr, "As Tech Booms, Workers Turn to Coding for Career Change," *New York Times*, July 28, 2015. www.nytimes.com.

23. Quoted in Royster, "Working with Big Data," p. 10.

24. Team Jigsaw, "5 Essential Skills Every Big Data Analyst Should Have," February 29, 2016. www.jigsawacademy.com.

25. Quoted in Royster, "Working with Big Data," p. 10.

26. Quoted in Royster, "Working with Big Data," p. 10.

27. Quoted in Royster, "Working with Big Data," p. 10.

28. Mina Farid, interview with the author, January 8, 2017.

Chapter 4: What Is It Like to Work as a Big Data Analyst?

29. Quoted in Dana Priest, "NSA Growth Fueled by Need to Target Terrorists," *Washington Post*, July 21, 2013. www.washingtonpost.com.

30. Quoted in Howard Baldwin, "Big Data's Big Impact Across Industries," *Forbes*, March 28, 2014. www.forbes.com.

31. Teradata, "Financial Services: A New Data-Driven Era for the Industry." http://bigdata.teradata.com.

32. Quoted in Marr, "The Most Practical Big Data Use Cases of 2016."

33. Quoted in Elena Malykhina, "Agencies See Big Data as Cure for Healthcare Ills," InformationWeek, March 26, 2014. www.informationweek.com.

34. Linda Burtch, *The Burtch Works Study: Salaries of Predictive Analytics Professionals*. Evanston, IL: Burtch Works, September 2016, pp. 4, 14.

Chapter 5: Advancement and Other Job Opportunities

35. Quoted in Qatar Is Booming, "Research Led by HBKU Scientists Offers a New Way of Identifying Brain Tumor Aggressiveness," February 15, 2016. www.qatarisbooming.com.
36. Quoted in Dan Bobkoff, "Seed by Seed, Acre by Acre, Big Data Is Taking Over the Farm," Business Insider, September 15, 2015.www.businessinsider.com.

Chapter 6: What Does the Future Hold for Big Data Analysts?

37. Morris, "The Sexiest Job of the 21st Century."
38. Quoted in Morris, "The Sexiest Job of the 21st Century."
39. Morris, "The Sexiest Job of the 21st Century."
40. Quoted in Kathryn Dill, "The Best Jobs for Work-Life Balance," *Forbes*, July 17, 2014. www.forbes.com.
41. Dill, "The Best Jobs for Work-Life Balance."
42. Quoted in *Economist*, "Data, Data Everywhere," February 25, 2010. www.economist.com.
43. Quoted in Antony Adshead, "Data Set to Grow 10-fold by 2020 as Internet of Things Takes Off," ComputerWeekly, April 9, 2014. www.computerweekly.com.
44. Maryanne Gaitho, "How Applications of Big Data Drive Industries," Simplilearn, October 20, 2015. www.simplilearn.com.

American Statistical Association (ASA)
732 N. Washington St.
Alexandria, VA 22314
website: www.amstat.org

Founded in 1839, the American Statistical Association is the second-oldest continuously operating professional association in the United States and the world's largest community of statisticians. The ASA supports excellence in the development, application, and dissemination of statistical science through meetings, publications, membership services, education, accreditation, and advocacy. Its website includes student resources and information on student competitions.

Association for Computing Machinery Special Interest Group on Management of Data (ACM SIGMOD)
2 Penn Plaza, Suite 701
New York, NY 10121
website: www.sigmod.org

The ACM SIGMOD is concerned with the principles, techniques, and applications of database management systems and data management technology. SIGMOD sponsors the annual SIGMOD/PODS conference, one of the most important and selective in the field. Its membership is open to students.

Data Management Association (DAMA) International
website: www.dama.org

DAMA International is a not-for-profit global association of technical and business professionals. Its educational programs are dedicated to advancing the concepts and practices of data management through research, education, publications, promotion of standards, and other activities.

EngineerGirl

National Academy of Engineering
500 Fifth St. NW, Room 1047
Washington, DC 20001
www.engineergirl.org

Created by the National Academy of Engineering, the Engineer-Girl website is designed to bring national attention to the exciting opportunities that engineering represents for girls and women. It features short profiles of 294 female engineers, including hardware, software, and database engineers. It also has dozens of in-depth interviews and areas devoted to "Ask an Engineer," "A Day in the Life," and "Historical Engineers."

Science Buddies

Sobrato Center for Nonprofits
560 Valley Way
Milpitas, CA 95035
website: www.sciencebuddies.org

Created to help students build their literacy in science and technology, the Science Buddies website contains more than fifteen thousand pages of scientist-developed subject matter (including experiments based on the latest academic research) and an on-line community of science professionals who volunteer to advise students. They also provide resources to support parents and teachers as they guide students doing hands-on science projects, including big data science projects.

PICTURE CREDITS

ABOUT THE AUTHOR

Bradley Steffens is an award-winning poet, playwright, novelist, and author of more than thirty nonfiction books for children and young adults. He is a two-time recipient of the San Diego Book Award for Best Young Adult and Children's Nonfiction: his *Giants* won the 2005 award, and his *J.K. Rowling* claimed the 2007 prize. Steffens also received the Theodor S. Geisel Award for best book by a San Diego County author in 2007.